PICASSO

BY GASTON DIEHL

CROWN TRADE PAPERBACKS - NEW YORK

Title page: SELF-PORTRAIT OF PICASSO, 1906
Museum of Art, Philadelphia

Series published under the direction of:
MADELEINE LEDIVELEC-GLOECKNER

Translated from the French by:
HELEN C. SLONIM

Copyright © 1977 by Bonfini Press Corporation, Naefels, Switzerland
All rights of reproduction of illustrations by S.P.A.D.E.M., Paris

Published by Crown Trade Paperbacks, 201 East 50th Street, New York, New York 10022.
Member of the Crown Publishing Group.

Random House, Inc. New York, Toronto, London, Sydney, Auckland

CROWN TRADE PAPERBACKS and colophon are trademarks of Crown Publishers, Inc.
Originally published in hardcover by Crown Publishers, Inc., in 1977.

Printed in Italy - Poligrafiche Bolis S.P.A., Bergamo

Library of Congress Cataloging-in-Publication is available upon request.

ISBN 0-517-88377-5

10 9 8 7 6 5 4 3 2 1

First Paperback Edition

THE FLOWER SELLER, 1901.   Oil, 14″ × 21″ (35.5 × 53.3 cm)
The Glasgow Art Gallery, Glasgow

I

FRUITFUL ENCOUNTERS

Satisfaction should be taken
where it is found, save in one's own work.
PICASSO

Nothing seems to cause greater prejudice than the habit, which has become a rule where Picasso is concerned, of breaking down and dismembering his work — under the pretense of explaining it — in as many periods as each particular biographer's fancy can discover. History cannot be burdened with these small detailed differences in order to judge what an artist really has achieved. Surely, most of these arbitrary decisions have lost all meaning as time has gone by. Bewildered in the labyrinth of overlapping and interwoven periods: blue, pink, African, green, Cubist, crystal, Romanesque, classic, Expressionist, Surrealist, tragic, intimist, etc..., the public only grasps a fragmentary aspect or a label, according to their own preferences.

This is why we thought it essential to consider Picasso's work in its integrity, to place it beyond the current classifications into which it would be useless to try and narrow it. Picasso's work is valid as

Waiting, 1900. Pastel. Madrid

a whole, through its fruitful diversity and unceasing renewal. Its extent, expanding over more than sixty years, demands that one should try to bring forward its unity of expression as contrasted to its diversity of appearances, these being explained by the period of time during which it was conceived.

However, before reaching the full possibility of his means — the rich complexity of which we will have to analyze — Picasso has known, from the beginning, how to profit from experiences or encounters which a favorable destiny put on his road. Why is this obstinately ignored when the painter himself never refused to recognize, even publicly, the debts he had made?

A STIMULATING FATHER

His father's influence was profound. Picasso has shown his appreciation by painting portraits and by affectionate ironic tales told to his friend Sabartès. As he started painting extremely young, there was some ground for the legend implying that he was self-taught, which seems to be common practice among modern artists. If at an age where others wonder about what they will do later, Picasso had already mastered his craft, he certainly owed it as much to his own dispositions as to an early initiation which was carried on according to the best tradition of the classic periods. José Ruiz Blasco, a needy artist, burdened by family obligations and mediocrity of successive jobs, took his revenge by dedicating himself to the education of his son, Pablo, born in 1881. The child's vocation had hardly emerged when his father put a paint brush in his hand, associated him with his work, and tried to make him share his passion for bull-fights and pigeons.

The results were astounding, and the young prodigy truly confirmed all his father's hopes. Picasso is eight years old when he sketches his first canvas; at twelve he can draw like Raphael, according to his own words, and acts as editor of a satiric paper. The teacher, well rewarded, can do no more than leave his palette in the hands of his pupil who, at the age of thirteen, begins a series of portraits which already show, as in his *Barefoot Girl*, a thorough understanding of Zurbarán or Velásquez. He considers the examinations at the Barcelona and Madrid art schools as mere jokes, and at sixteen is already reaping laurels from the fashionable salons.

To reward his father's effort and advice, he could look forward to an outstanding academic career, but an instinctive spirit of independence pushed him to refuse any guidance for the future. However, at intervals, a certain leaning toward classicism recalls the mark left during his first steps.

THE SEDUCTIONS OF BARCELONA

Back to this town in April 1889, after a long convalescence at Horta de Ebro, the new sphere in which he dwells definitely turns him from the road he had followed up to then. At this period he draws with passion, sketching portraits of his companions who soon become his faithful friends and who has welcomed him to the "4 Gats," a pale replica of Bruant's Cabaret. In the atmosphere of Barcelona, which feeds the ambitious dissipations of Gaudí, an obsolete symbolism mingling Nietzche, Wagner, Ibsen with the English or German Preraphaelites, still prevails. There is plenty to quench the curiosity and greed of a youth for new horizons. Working in Cardona Ituro's studio, Picasso gets to know Overbeck's works. In the magazine "Joventud" where he illustrates decadent poems, he is in a position to appreciate the art of Arnold Böcklin, Aubrey Beardsley, Edward Burnes-Jones or Edvard Münch. Miguel Utrillo makes him share his admiration for El Greco, and he is familiar with the Japanese crepons, as can be seen from his *Portrait of Lola*.

Far from neglecting these numerous possibilities, a slow incubation sets in which will later bring him to choose an insistant linear mannerism and a disillusioned philosophy of life, strengthened by the painful circumstances through which he is then going. For the time being, he is exasperated by an insidious impatience which is reflected in numerous drawings and pastels where the face of the world he is discovering is drawn with the bitter spontaneity already shown in some previous canvases: *Interior of a Café, The Gypsy Girl*. The atmosphere in which he lives strikes him as heavy. He has already realized that he has nothing more to hope for and dreams, like so many of his companions, of going to seek the exhortations and recognition of Paris. The Universal Exhibition of 1900 will give him the opportuniry.

Seated Woman, 1906. Pen and ink. Former Collection of Gertrude Stein

SEATED NUDE, 1902. Oil, 18⅛″ × 23⅝″ (46 × 60 cm)
Private Collection, Paris

BULLFIGHT, 1901
Oil, 19″ × 22″ (48.2 × 56 cm)
Collection Max Pellequer, Paris

▷

ACROBAT ON A BALL, 1904-1905
Oil, 58″ × 39″ (147.5 × 99.2 cm)
Museum of Modern Art, Moscow

HARLEQUIN AND HIS COMPANION, 1901.   Oil, 28¾″ × 23¼″ (73 × 59 cm)
Museum of Modern Art, Moscow

MATERNITY, 1903.   Pastel, 18″ × 16″ (45.7 × 40.6 cm).   Museum of Modern Art, Barcelona

THE EMBRACE, 1900.   Oil, 20½″ × 21⅝″ (52 × 55 cm).   Museum of Modern Art, Moscow

LITTLE GIRL WITH A BASKET OF
FLOWERS, 1905
Oil, 61″ × 29″ (155 × 73.7 cm)
Former Collection Gertrude Stein

SEATED NUDE, 1905.   Oil.   Museum of Modern Art, Paris

Head of a Woman, 1905. Pen and wash drawing

Two months later he is back in Spain, having managed to sell some of his work to the dealer Berthe Weill and to arouse the interested support of his compatriot Mañac. Full of ambitious plans, he settles down in Madrid, starts the magazine "Arte Joven" with the writer Francisco de Assis Saler, but he soon goes back to Barcelona and then again to Paris.

How come this young nineteen-year old boy has the impetuosity to make him discover Fauvism before its time? How come he is so sure of himself? How come he is possessed with such a fever for work that he can present, almost simultaneously, a pastel exhibition at Paradès, and an impressive array of seventy-five of his works at Ambroise Vollard, in June 1901?

He found a tacit acknowledgement of his dearest aspirations in all that Paris had to show him, even more than in Nonell's encouragements. He tries to grasp and remember everything: Posters by Jules Chéret or Henri de Toulouse-Lautrec which he tears off the walls, works by Edgar Degas and Auguste Renoir and by his nearest contemporaries such as Giovanni Boldini, Pierre Bonnard and Maurice Denis, glanced at during exhibitions, and also T.A. Steinlein whose work he knows through "The Illustrated Gil Blas." Following their examples, sometimes even taking up again their themes or methods directly, he transcribes quickly, but with a sharpness which is already typical, the same café-concert shows, dances, night-life, horse races, interiors, or deep perspectives of streets, in a happy colored blossoming, where the shapes are diluted in suggestive blots, hardly outlined by darker colors: *The Flower Seller, Moulin de la Galette, Boulevard de Clichy, The Cancan, Longchamps, The Diners, Woman with Make-Up, Woman with Dog, Woman Washing*, etc... He has barely started along this way when, with sudden revulsion, he abandons it for ever.

The happy liveliness of tones disappears to be replaced by dull harmonies, and even more often by blue monochrome painting. The gay life of the streets vanishes into the darkness of night. We enter a closed, silent, strange world, almost an hallucination, where hungry-looking figures, with elongated limbs and distressed dazed looks — harlequins, prostitutes, miserable couples, beggars, old men or women — seem to await, prostrated, some improbable redemption. Until the end of 1904, Picasso's work will be "this damp painting, blue like the wet bottom of the abyss, and pitiful" to take the definition which Guillaume Apollinaire gave later.

There is a certain excess of youth in this desire for maceration, in this exclusive choice of themes where Barcelona's experiences can be found through the allegoric figurations and artificial social sentimentality. Some paintings, however, show a real melancholy, almost a bitter resignation: *Harlequin and His Companion, Women at the Bar, Women Sitting, The Outcasts, The Meal of the Blind, The Old Jew, The Two Sisters, The Couple, Maternity*. This painful expression of life is not a pose. His exhibition at Vollard was very discouraging, bringing him only the poet Max Jacob's friendship. His former companion, Casamegas, commits suicide; this memory obsesses the painter: *Death, Evocation, Life*. He is also disillusioned by the big city. The "little Goya" who had enjoyed an enthusiastic welcome, is being forgotten and suffers from loneliness.

When he is in Barcelona, as well as in Paris, he has the same feeling of being in a strange land, of being a wanderer, rejected by those who had helped him before, reduced to living in sordid rooms, needy and desperate. However, difficulties and lack of money only affect him superficially and his passion for work is never quelled. The almost simultaneous meeting with Paul Gauguin's and Vincent

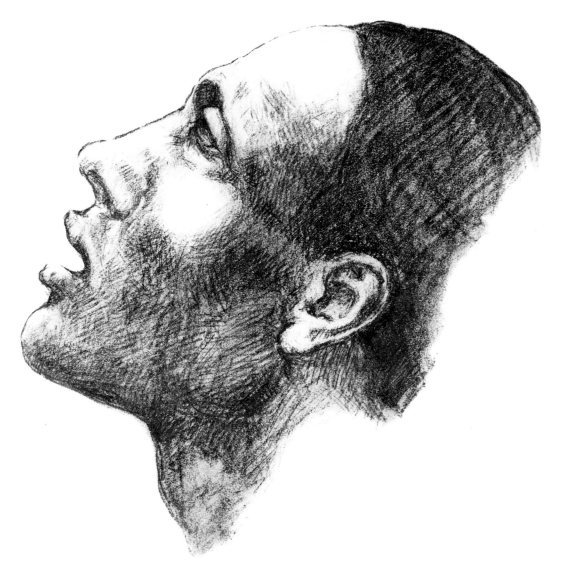

The Blind Man, 1902.   Pencil.   Paris

van Gogh's work, upsets him thoroughly — he says so himself — hastens his evolution and helps him emerge to his real self.   As soon as he had arrived in Paris, in June 1901, he had been able to see almost all of the famous Van Gogh retrospective, opened a month earlier at Bernheim's, which also had such a deep influence on Vlaminck and Matisse.   A little later, in December, he meets a compatriot, Paco Durio, a faithful admirer and friend of Gauguin's, is introduced to the latter's circle and spends whole evenings talking about Gauguin, about Tahiti, the poem Noa-Noa, and Charles Morice.

Where else, if not from this double influence, would he have found the attitude which is now his, of expressive lines and decisive contours (*Child and Pigeon, Seated Nude*, of elongation and systematic distortions which he will keep for some time (*Woman with Crow*, 1904; *Woman with Fan*, 1905) and

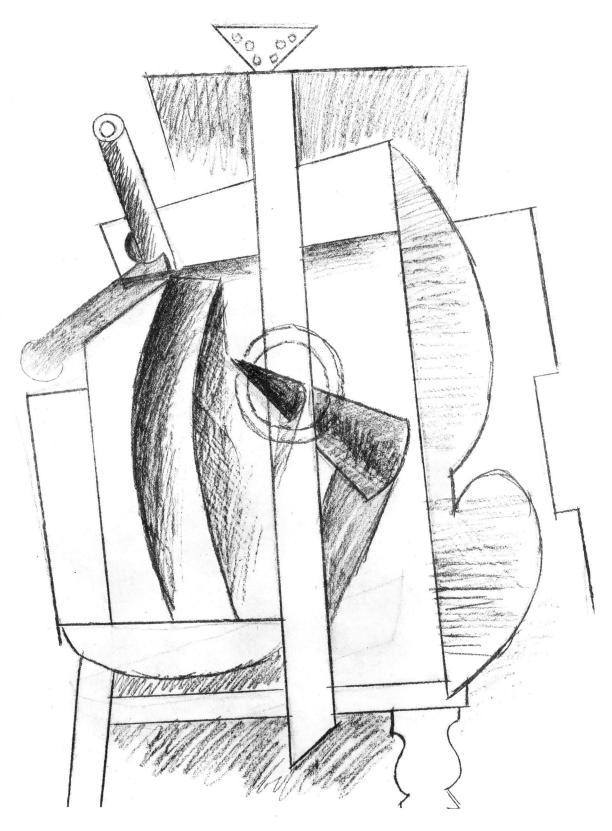

Violin and Flute, 1913.   Pencil.   Paris

HEAD OF A WOMAN, 1907. Oil, 33″ × 36″ (84 × 91.5 cm). Collection André Lefèvre, Paris

STUDY FOR THE DEMOISELLES D'AVIGNON, 1906.   Gouache.   Private collection, Paris

STUDY FOR THE DEMOISELLES D'AVIGNON, 1907. Gouache. Private collection, Paris

PORTRAIT OF BIBI LA PURÉE, 1901. Oil, 22″ × 15″ (56 × 38 cm). Collection Max Pellequer, Paris

Three-quarter Head, 1908.   Pencil.   Paris

even this almost symbolic use of blue which, according to Sabartès' true appreciation "is a yearning toward something higher amidst despair and sadness"? Surely he remembers Van Gogh in certain themes on loneliness which semm directly borrowed from that artist: *At the Café*, *Squatting Women*, *The Absinth Drinkers*, *The Bock*, *Reclining Drinking Woman*, or from Gauguin in certain typical forms of composition: *Life*, *The Two Sisters*. Beyond the immediate effect, his almost daily meetings with Gauguin influences his future. In April 1904 he settles down in Paco Durio's studio at the "Bateau Lavoir" when he comes back to Paris for the fourth time to remain. It drives him to discover, at the Ethnographic Museum, Polynesian primitive art which, as he so often outlined, will initiate the plastic revolution he introduced in 1907.

In the meantime the moulding stage is coming to a triumphal end in the years 1905 and 1906. He now has friends who support him: Guillaume Apollinaire, Maurice Raynal, André Salmon. The presence of a woman at his side, excites his desire to strengthen his conquests, and awakes his sensuality: *Harlequin's Family*, *Study for the Harem*, *Seated Nude*, *Nude with Tight Hair*, *Woman Washing Herself*.

His canvases show a sort of smile opening on cheerful horizons and illuminated by the sweetness of pink and rainbow hued tints (*Bathing Horses*). In the dawn of this new day breaking out in his work, mountebanks, tumblers and circus people — which he is continuously seeing as a neighbor at the Medrano Circus — make a last parade before heartily disappearing on the road: *Girl on a Ball*, *The Athlete*, *Family of Acrobats*, *The Jugglers*.

Starting now, Picasso deliberately settles himself in the midst of life. Abandoning his familiar half-dreamed shapes, he looks searchingly at the husky women of Schoorl (*The Dutchwoman*, 1905), or at his models (*Little Girl with Flower Basket*), or at the proud gait of the peasant-women of Gosol: *Woman with Bread*, *Hair Setting*, 1906. He scrutinizes all the faces around him, including his own: *Fernando Oliveiro*, *Gertrude Stein*, *Self-Portrait*. He loads his palette vigorously with harsh ochres, hardens and condenses his line up to the point of sometimes making it knotty or angular, strongly accentuates the relief — for he is interested in sculpture and also tries his hand at this form of art: *Harlequin*, 1905; *Head*, 1906; *Head of a Woman* and *Mask*, 1907.

Without surrendering any part of his inner-self he finally won the battle, and, at the age of twenty-five, managed victoriously to impose himself on Paris. Becoming more sympathetic, Vollard quickly buys a whole stack of Picasso's canvases. A small group of collectors follows him: Leo and Gertrude Stein, the Russian Shchukin, Wilhelm Udhe. Soon Daniel Kahnweiler offers him a contract. But the spirit of adventure takes hold of Picasso and carries him away.

II

THE BEGINNING OF AN UNCEASING INVENTORY

> *I don't work from nature, but*
> *in front of and with nature.*
> PICASSO

During the winter 1906-1907 Picasso gives his work a decisive turn. This is no coincidence. How could an African statue, seen at Gertrude Stein's in Matisse's hands, be sufficient to start up this new trend? The numerous preliminary studies he makes for *The Demoiselles d'Avignon*, and for all his

Reclining Nude, 1914. Black-lead drawing. Paris

following canvases, show that he is working in a well determined direction and that he has deliberately and knowingly broken with his former style.

Why should he have chosen this time? Simply because he senses that he has fully mastered his craft and feels free to start an ambitious and long-term plan, which, as we will see, will easily fill his whole life. Now he already knows that he has managed to overcome the instinctive virtuosity of his hand from which the line just flows, as seen in the works prior to the so-called blue period and even more in the later paintings with their gaily blossoming tones where fancy smartness was deteriorating into an empty refined mannerism. Breaking with this past, he himself qualifies it without ambiguity to one of his friends, in October 1906: "All that was just sentimentality." Moreover, he has found in the pictorial inheritance which his epoch offered him, the necessary basis for feeding and justifying his plan. For the same reasons as the Impressionists, Van Gogh, Gauguin, Georges Seurat or Paul Cézanne, he wants to tackle the main problem which is to pull painting out of its routine and obsolete rules in order to hand it back its personal language, to release a new harmony between expression of forms, organization of space and the structure of rhythms.

So many artists had preceded him in this search: how to proceed from visual perception to pictorial design, from the image of nature to its plastic transcription. But Picasso is the first to have realized with outstanding clearness that a double, closely linked inventory must be made of the visible world on the one hand and the means of transcription on the other. Trying to establish these correlations, he soon discovers — and there too he is the first to do so — that he must henceforth free himself from any imitative or illusionary art if he wants his canvases to show a world which is entirely thought out and recreated by himself. Those two assumptions, set down and put into practice by Picasso with a judgement which is the mark of his genius, were destined to revolutionize painting and to dominate almost all the experiments which have been undertaken up to now. Thanks to Picasso the artist recovers his natural role of inventor, of a small god, creator of new worlds. Those assumptions were far from being arbitrary; they gradually dawned upon his attention while he was making empiric explorations, which he has the rare merit of having carried on with a quiet obstinacy. Without judging beforehand the results he will achieve, his attitude commands by the risks he was running but was by no means sure he would win; he knew in advance that he had to expect incomprehension or desertion even by his best friends. He clearly defined his attitude: "Nothing can be done without loneliness. I have created for myself a loneliness which nobody suspects. It is very difficult, nowadays, to be alone." The proof of his sincerity is in the number of experiments he made, introducing in the natural development of his work so many unexpected modifications or apparent contradictions; these are the despair awakening of some of his biographers and of his imitators.

Around some main idea that has come into his mind, or as the result of outside circumstances awakening his curiosity or exciting his sensitivity — trip to Rome in 1917, "Mercure" ballet in 1924, attraction of Surrealism in 1928, settling down at Boisgeloup in 1931, the Spanish civil war in 1936, the Second World War, the Liberation of France, visits to Antibes in 1946, — he proceeds, during several months and sometimes even several years, with systematic experiments which he patiently develops to their extreme limits.

INITIATING A NEW GRAMMAR OF SHAPES

The bewildering multiplicity of these endeavors has, nevertheless, a common ground, around which they can be classified, and which often partially justifies them: Picasso's everlasting desire, as his own notes confirm, to make a permanent inventory of all the shapes which exist in Nature. Few artists

SEATED WOMAN, 1909. Oil, 38″ × 42″ (96.5 × 106.7 cm)
Collection Roland, London ▷

28

MAN WITH A
MANDOLIN, 1912
Oil, 16″ × 24″
(40.5 × 61 cm)
Collection Mattioli
Milan

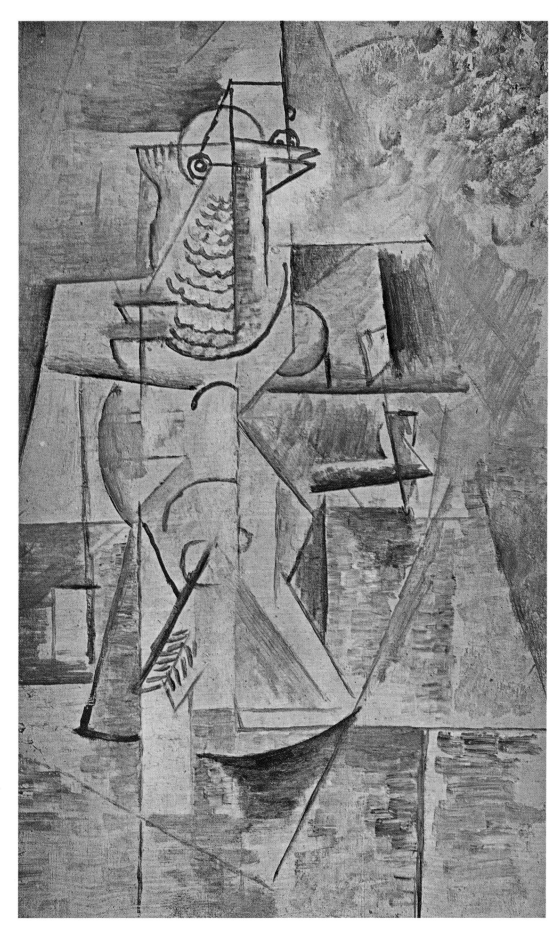

WOUNDED BIRD
1911, Oil
Collection
Paul Chadourne
Paris

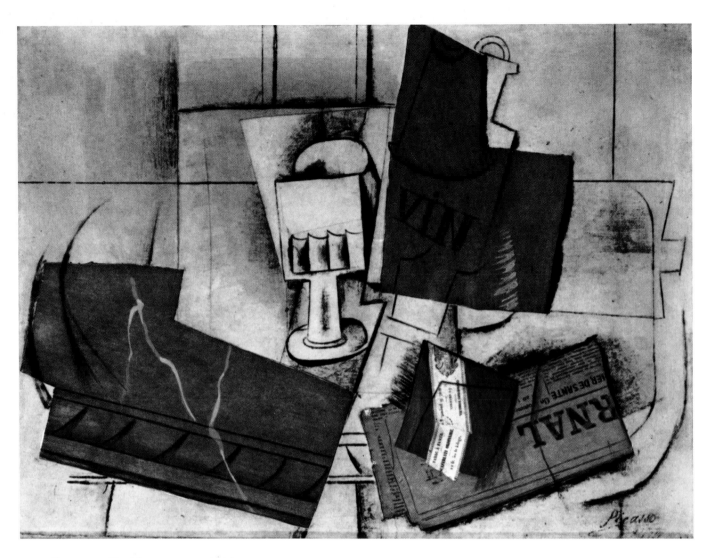

COLLAGE: THE JOURNAL, ca 1914
22″ × 29″ (56 × 73.7 cm)
Collection Dalsace, Paris

▷

THE BALCONY, 1919
Oil, 15″ × 11½″ (38 × 29.2 cm)
Private collection

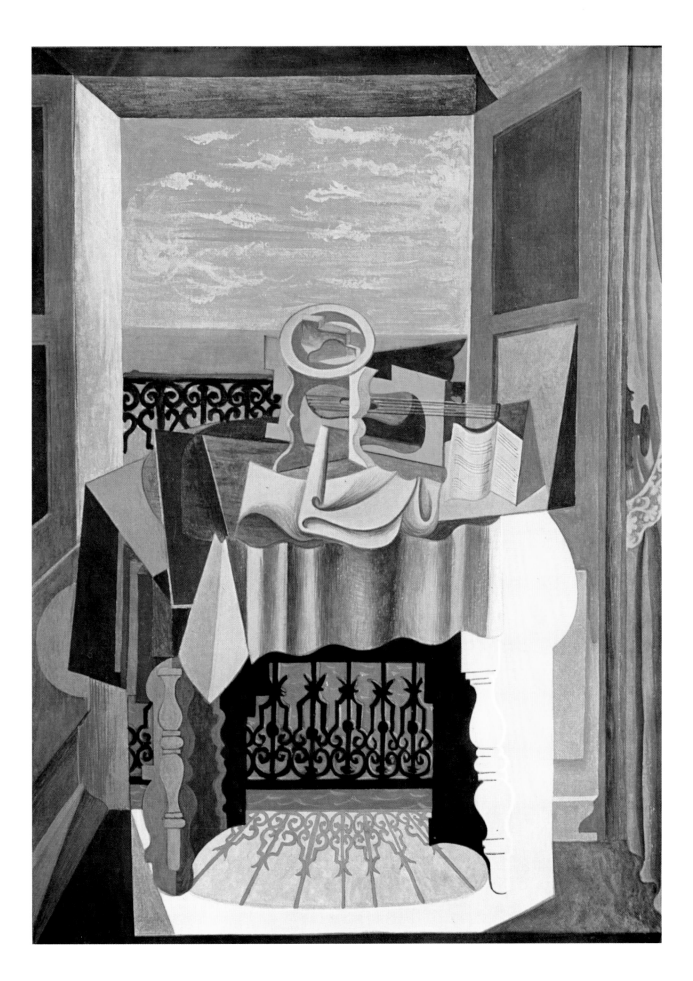

PIERROT, 1918.   Oil, 36½″ × 28¾″ (92.7 × 73 cm).   Museum of Modern Art, New York. Sam Lewisohn Bequest

ITALIAN GIRL, 1917.   Oil, 64″ × 48″ (162.5 × 122 cm).   Emil G. Buehrle Foundation, Zurich

STILL LIFE, 1923.   Oil.   Collection Mrs. A. D. Lasker, New York

The Three Acrobats, 1925. India ink. Paris

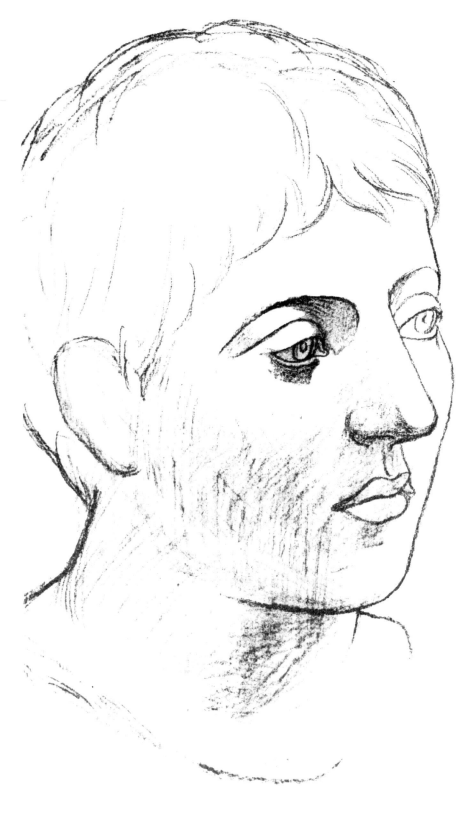

Head of a Young Man, 1923. Pencil. Paris

Head of a Woman, 1921.   Pastel.   Fontainebleau

have explored in this path as far as he has; practically nothing has evaded his queries which have gradually spread to the visible or invisible universe itself, including human beings, landscapes, objects and elements of the vegetable, mineral or animal kingdom. From one to another, depending on circumstances, his curiosity expands, catching, as it goes by, fantasms, dreams, and most unwonted evocations as well as traditional mythological representations. Even from shapes which he has analyzed to their minutest details — face or body of a woman, guitar, bull, horse, owl, — he seems to draw on an unceasing renewal of his imagination and weaves an infinite embroidery with astounding graphic interpretations.

Despite what has been said about him, Picasso is never experimenting just for the fun of it and knows when to stop, just before falling into decorative art. Little by little in work which he takes up again and again and transforms, by means of distortions, he associates more closely the whole of the optic, tactile and mobile sensations — very often he proceeds to parallel studies in sculpture — and he always slowly approaches the shapes before absorbing them entirely, decanting and condensing them into a symbolic design. He is both persevering and enthusiastic in this task. In this connection one remembers with emotion a little series of still lifes, painted around 1908-1909, seen at Roger Dutilleul's, sweet, fresh and pearl-like, where Picasso had assembled humble elements: fruit, bread, cake, fish, accentuating from canvas to canvas his soaring toward a quiet purity of structures reduced to their essentials and set together with fervor.

His authority is of the same sort on this complete idiom of elliptic shapes which he has made his own and endowed with such exceptional potentiality of expression that most of them have finally imposed themselves on our whole epoch. He can make them go through every possible "metamorphosis" to use his own word, without detaching them from himself. He frequently achieves astonishing results, obtaining interchangeable shapes by the sole means of conferring a sort of unexpected representative quality to some odd stone, root or pieces of metal. This method has nowadays been dangerously generalized, as have so many other things borrowed from his creative genius. Whatever the appearance might be, this is no trick by chance; Picasso has always shown an anxiety to probe simultaneously every possibility of matter. There also, nothing will be left aside. From his early days, he makes use of sculpture, and soon also of engraving, going through all the means by which he achieves surprising effects: *The Frugal Meal*, 1904, treated in etching; the series *The Mountebanks* 1905, in drypoint etching; the first wood engravings in 1906 and a little later the lithograph.

One day, seemingly at the suggestion of Braque with whom he works at Céret during the summer of 1911, he discovers that some elements can be given sufficient expressive value: printers letters, wood substitutes. Pounding enthusiastically upon this principle, he is going to undertake an almost systematic investigation of all the substitute products which can be incorporated into painting or can animate surfaces. In turn he will use sand, fragments of newspaper, wallpaper, posters or cloth, visiting cards, etc... and will impart to them the possibility of becoming a living presence, of transforming themselves into expressive flat tints, in those famous "pasted papers" of the years 1912-1914 which have now been promoted to the renk of masterpiece due to their sober power. During that period he operates in the same fashion with a few sculptures which have more correctly been called "constructions" and are simple combinations of pieces of wood. Later in 1924 he makes use of wire and iron rods for decorating the ballet "Mercure," and will soon start, with the help of Julio Gonzales, his first lattice-sculptures. Then, he brings into his work the figurative participation of all the rubbish he can find, from sack cloth to feather duster or bicycle saddle. Matter, whatever it may be, cannot remain lifeless in his hands; he seems to force his own vitality into it and more recently one could see the admirable use he has made of lithography or ceramic.

▷

40

PORTRAIT OF THE SON OF THE ARTIST AS PIERROT, 1924
Oil, 51¼″ × 31¾₁₆″ (130 × 79.2 cm)
Collection of the artist

THREE MUSICIAN, 1921
Oil, 6′ 7″ × 7′ ¾″ (200.7 × 222.9 cm)
The Museum of Modern Art, New York
Mrs. Simon Guggenheim Fund

◁

TWO HARLEQUINS, 1919
Oil, 10⅛″ × 7¾″ (25.7 × 17 cm)
Collection Gilbert W. Chapman, New York

43

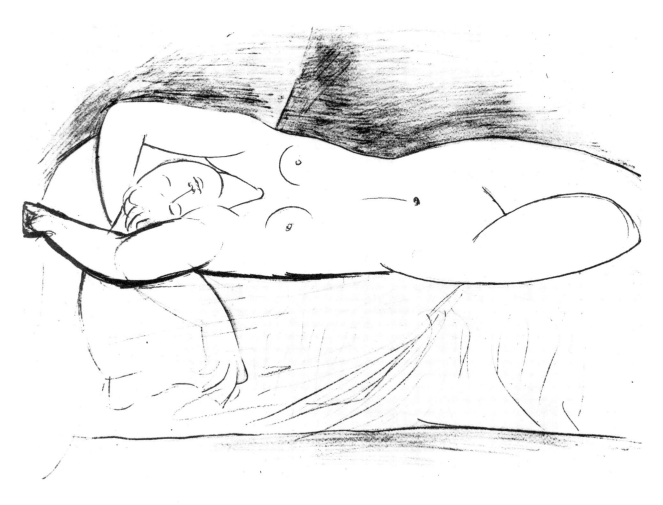

Reclining Nude, 1931.   Black lead.   Paris

IN STATING THE LAWS OF A RHYTHMIC CONSTRUCTION

Although appearing to be an eccentric, Picasso follows a rigorously composed action, closely associating sensations and intelligence and eschewing any useless dispersion.   His expressive drive never ceases to depend on his will to organize a work of art plastically and simultaneously to solve harmoniously the problems of disposition, space, color and rhythm; he is determined to verify and index the various means of transcription by his own efforts.   He pursues this examination so scrupulously and persistently that the soundness of his efforts is occasionally deceiving and at first leads one to think that he must have started from some doctrinal basis.

That was the case with the so-called Cubist formula into which, despite his denials and constant struggle to protect himself from the hold of any system, the public has long wanted to enclose Picasso.   It matters little that Polynesian masks or Iberic Romanesque sculptures were the origin of his first trials at schematizing human features or bodies which is first introduced in his faces in 1907 and is shown with magnificent impudence in *The Demoiselles d'Avignon*.   Far from any dogmatic spirit he tries an

◁

WOMAN ASLEEP: THE DREAM, 1932
Oil, 59″ × 44″ (150 × 111.8 cm)
Collection W. Ganz, New York

45

Boisgeloup, 1932.   India ink and oil

expressive simplification of contours and masses, inspired sometimes by Seurat's precedent, and especially by Cézanne's, whose large retrospective at the Salon d'Automne of 1907 is destined to stimulate and temporarily direct his thoughts: *Landscape with Two Faces* and *The Cronstadt*, 1908; *The Factory* and *Reservoir at Horta de Ebro*, 1909.

But he proceeds by groping with no initial theory; he cuts down to essential shapes and planes (*Little House in a Garden*, 1908), rejects the modulations of tones which Cézanne liked so much and restricts for a long period his palette to a few earth colors to make the luminous contrast come out better. If, in the company of Braque with whom he works until the war, he makes use of the geometrical decomposition of volumes, neither of them thinks of considering this as an end in itself, and they will both abandon it in 1910, precisely at the time where the supporters of Cubism adopt it as an exclusive principle.   Unlike these people, Picasso always relies on direct visual observation and, as Pierre Frascatel has so conclusively demonstrated, he always starts by "studying with an infinite patience the phenomena of close vision"; then in turn he discovers "the association under new angles of very close parts of the visible world," as already shown in the still lifes or portraits of the years 1909, 1910, as well as in the related visual distortions which he will use after the war. Examples are his series of *Women on the Seashore*, (1920), with their monstruous deformations; his multi-leveled faces, which appear in 1928 or, starting in 1937, his cruel portraits with their multiple profiles. Soon he also tries "to make use of the rapidity of substitution of fragments of visions on the retina."

In order to grasp better "the immediate fundamental sensations," he multiplies optical and tactile experiments, contacts with matter itself in sculpture corresponding exactly to his painting (*Woman's Head*, 1909, *The Glass of Absinth* or *Mandolin*, 1914). This will induce him, at a later date, to make exactly the opposite test; that is to evoke from a number of his canvases masses of carved or sculptured blocks of anthropomorphic aspect; *Bathing Girl*, 1928, *Silhouette by the Sea*, 1929; *Silhouette*; *Woman Sitting on the Beach*, 1937.

Let us not think, however, that there is the slightest place in his mind for scientific consideration, whether he forces himself to use some strict method of investigation or, according to the legend spread by Apollinaire and his friends of the Golden Section, whether he becomes enthusiastic about higher

Boisgeloup, 1932. India ink

mathematics or applications of the fourth dimension. Is it not only from observation that he gets the idea of displaced and interpenetrating planes which will lead him to abandon geometrical perspective? Is it not from pacing around his model, as any sculptor would, and registering successive impressions that he deduces the principle of simultaneous points of view of the same object or of fragmentation of various objects glanced at? Nevertheless, his main interest is in the major problem of creation which he instinctively chose: Combine and assemble various pictorial elements, obtain their true junction on the canvas, attain the internal unity of painting (which Cézanne had already defined) and achieve a degree of cohesion which enables him to associate the whole universe, throwing down frontiers or traditional distinction between man and all that is surrounding him.

All his researches get more precise during the particulary fruitful years 1907-1917. New rules are set up which will become of common use both for himself and many contemporary artists: elimination of any reference to conventional perspective of lighting effect with their particular tones; dissociation of contours as a whole toward particular parts or fragments, the presence of which is underlined; achievement of a specific pictorial space which respects the surface of the canvas.

He is especially eager to release and reinforce the structure of a work so that it can play a leading part. We can see him, with an almost Cartesian logic during the admirable progressive experimenting period before the 1914 war, start by accentuating the main lines and volumes, then go to a crystal-like demultiplication of the levels, themselves divided in many luminous facets and thus already attain a melodious architecture of fragmentary shapes, imbricated, mounted one onto another often disolving into a meticulously arranged, subtely modulated fractionization. Pursuing an ever more absolute simplification, he ends by a rigorous regrouping of distinct flat tints which in fact are linked and carefully distributed for the general effect in conformity with an equilibrium process which will often from now on, serve as the basis to his painting.

He may later introduce many modifications to enrich and differentiate the texture itself of the various colored splashes (*Still Life Painted on Red Paper*, 1914, *The Italian Girl*, 1917), he may preferably direct his efforts toward an ingenious willful fragmentation of surfaces (*Jug and Fruit Bowl*, 1931), or even sometimes chose an extreme bareness to the limit of etching (*The Studio*, 1927-28; *The Kitchen*, 1948) or of strict construction (*Project for a Monument*, 1929); he will never fail to tighten the structure and to underline its monument-like nature.

In this adjusting conception, which goes singularly further than the elementary geometry of the beginnings, another factor also emerges with the utmost efficacy: his desire to integrate movement into composition, to set down the problem of rhythm and enrich the work of art with the qualities of a real live organism. This aim certainly guides his research even more than speculations on space, barely started in 1909-1910, and for which he merely exercises his reflexes instead of submitting himself to some meticulous reasoning. He dedicates himself to this in answer to his own instinctive dynamism and will always carefully watch its successful extension.

Even before 1914, rhythm is the master, punctuating each work with a discreet pounding by the play of orthogonal criss-crosses, less frequently oblique, which grow quicker and soon extend into multiple echos, thanks to their clever repetition up to infinity; Piet Mondrian will turn this method into a real formula. But already Picasso, to avoid insidious monotony, demands the utmost autonomy for both line and colored splash in order to obtain an intensive suggestion of movement by the simple alternated juxtaposition of planes and the free fragmentation of shapes.

Le Coq, 1938.   Pastel, 30½″ × 21¼″ (77.5 × 54 cm).   Collection Mr. and Mrs. Ralph Colin, New York

STILL LIFE, 1914 (Painted on Red Paper)
23″ × 29″ (58.5 × 73.7 cm)
Collection Flechtheim, Berlin

STILL LIFE WITH BUST AND PALETTE, 1925
Oil, 38¼″ × 51¼″ (97 × 130 cm)
Private collection, New York

Young Girl
1937
India ink
Paris

Under the influence of the ballets to which he has been invited to collaborate, "Parade" in 1917, "The Tricorne" in 1919, "Pulcinella" in 1920, "Cuadro Flamenco" in 1921, "Mercure" in 1924, and of the musicians whom he frequently sees, Igor Stravinsky, Manuel de Falla, Darius Milhaud, Eric Satie, as well as that of a dancer who lives with him, Picasso adopts a sequence of theories, particularly daring from the pictorial point of view, which he will lucidly follow to their ultimate corollaries. Before the series *Bathing Girls*, 1920 and 1921, the arabesque appears more and more frequently in his canvases and soon boldly inscribes its curvilinear rhythms; these in turn give birth to curved spaces and volumes.

Sometimes they soar impetuously, leap in short disjointed jumps and abrupt jolts (*The Dance*, 1929) or meander in an uninterrupted lace-work of feverish sinuosities on which are projected like some flashing cut-outs that bring to mind the syncopated rhythm of jazz or motion pictures in the extraordinary series: *The Painter and His Model*, 1926 and 1927. Sometimes the scintillation is toned down, develops like a symphony the powerful network of its interlaced design (*The Milliner's Workshop*, 1926) giving way to the melody of sinuosity interwoven in sweet cadence (*Sitting Women*, 1927; *The Dream*, 1932), developing into a billowy sequence of volutes (*Still Life on Small Table*, 1931) or to spirals blended into a flexible abstract calligraphy (Illustration for "An Unknown Masterpiece" by Balzac, 1931).

This, however, did not stop his experiments on the effects of mobility of planes which he made use of in decorations or costumes for ballets. He will use it more and more with every available means: balancing of flat tints with vigorous chromatic oppositions intensified by an independent graphism (*Violinist*, 1918; *The Chimney*, 1920), overlapping of planes or simultaneous intersection at sharp angles and triangular fractionization of surfaces (*The Guitar*, 1920); *The Three Musicians*). The dynamism of the whole work is often emphasized by interposing sinuous curves, festoons, saw teeth (*The Balcony*, 1919), or in the series *The Open Window*, 1924, and sometimes by the repetition of vertical rhythm: *Two Women at the Window*, 1927, which can be found still later in *Boats on the Beach*, 1937 or *The Bay of Cannes*, 1958.

Keeping a Total Freedom of Choice

Far from ending his bold forays into such scarcely accessible ground and limiting himself to exploiting one or another of the channels he developed and restricting himself to some well marked road, as his pretended supporters and disciples begged him to do after his magnificent 1932 exhibition, up to these last years, Picasso had never ceased to expand the field of his activities and researches.

Even less than before he never proceeds merely seeking adventure. With his characteristic obstinacy, despite appearances, he works with an undeniable spirit of continuity, draws every consequence from former trials, makes use of whatever he has learned in the past to vary the plastic organization of shapes and colors, to extend their power of meaning, to multiply the complex combinations of rhythmic structures so as to be able to respond each time to the diversity of the needs for expression.

Following a habit acquired long ago, he simultaneously conducts several diverging or opposed experiments, takes up the same problem again after a few year or, just for fun, weaves an infinity of variations around a single motif. This makes it almost impossible to classify chronologically the innumerable detours and trends of Picasso's mind. For example, the theme of the Minotaur is already strongly present in the series of 1933 etchings and appears as a mysterious symbol in 1935 in the famous engraving *Minotauromachie*. Similarly, a cruelly virulent schematism settles down in the various bull races painted

Minotaur and His Prey, 1936.   Pen and ink

in 1934 after the returned from Spain and lashes out with magnificent force in the series of eighteen etchings, *Songe et Mensonge de France*, beginning of 1937.   Almost right after that he can synthesize it in a painting where his epic lyricism and dynamism expand freely, *Guernica*, all the more easily as the rhythmic arrangement and even the grisaille seem, at the monumental level, to recapitulate the plastic solutions foreseen ten years before in *The Milliner's Workshop*.   When he wants to do it again in a calmer atmosphere in 1945 with *Le Charnier* the painting will remain unfinished.

As has been pointed out, no doubt the dramatic tension of the pre-war period is apparent, directly or indirectly, in a great part of his work: tortured heads with hideous distortions (*Weeping Woman*, 1937) lashed and fearful faces (*Man or Woman with Lollipop*, 1938); disarticulated faces with double profiles (series of *Sitting Women*, 1937 to 1944); monstrous bodies (*Nude Woman Combing Her Hair*, 1940); or through an aggressive, sharp-angled, geometricization with prismatic contractions enhanced

The Conversation, 1938.   India ink.   Paris

STILL LIFE WITH HEAD OF A BLACK BULL, 1938
Oil, 38″ × 51″ (96.5 × 129.5 cm)
Private collection

STILL LIFE, 1923
Oil, 44″ × 34″ (111.8 × 86.5 cm)
Museum of Modern Art, Paris

Skull of a Sheep, 1939.   Gouache and wash drawing.   Collection of the artist

by the harshness of contrasts with dominating greens and violets: *Night Fishing at Antibes*, 1939; series of *Lying Nudes*, and numerous still lifes painted at that period as well as a series of *View of Paris*, 1945. But if he attained his paroxysm at this period it must be granted that his system of over-emphasized deformations and triangular alterations correspond to a frequent characteristic which is part of Picasso's graphism.   It can be found in 1926 (*Woman's Head*) and in 1948 (*Sitting Woman*) or in 1956 (*Two Nude Women*), or again as applied to people whom he undeniably loves: *Portrait of Maïa*, 1938 *Sabartès as a Hidalgo*, 1939; *Claude and Paloma*, 1950.   Later he blossoms out into colored fireworks regulated by an extraordinary graphic dexteriy: *The Demoiselles on the Banks of the Seine*, 1950; *Women of Algiers*, 1955.

In contrast an unexpected clearing opens up with *La Joie de Vivre*, 1946 where the dancing sinuosities, the coolness of colors expanding in large alternated planes, compose a true song of happiness which becomes duller and less convincing when he tries it again in his *Hymn to Peace*, 1952, or in *Bathing*, 1958-1959, at the UNESCO building in Paris, which is more extended in the manner of a frieze.   During the winter 1950-1951 he gives very remote versions of the landscape at Vallauris: *Panorama at Vallauris*

◁

SKULL OF A BULL, 1942.   Oil, 54″ × 38″ (130 × 97 cm)
Private collection, Paris

GUERNICA, 1937
Oil, 11′ 5½″ × 25′ 5¾″ (349.3 × 776.6 cm)
Picasso Museum, Barcelona

Dove, 1942.   Wash drawing.   Paris

lines, *Smoke at Vallauris* describing the meticulous arrangement of the roofs in tiers. The dozen portraits of Sylvette David, executed in May-June 1954, also offer the extreme scale of plastic variations starting with direct notation and ending with free harmonic arrangement.

Indeed Picasso enjoys passing from one idiom to another, with a quiet breeziness which will always disconcert his followers. Sometimes he likes to revert to the sole demands of a classical craftmanship which he has completely mastered as soon as he comes to Paris he pays frequent visits to the Louvre to compare his own draftmanship to that of Jean-Dominique Ingres. Very soon his ability almost becomes an exercise of style as he mingles it in turn with what he has learnt about space, structure or rhythm. Starting with the still painstakingly done portraits of his youth, the *Soler Family*, 1903 or *Jaimes Sabartès*, 1904, we reach the spurting and free line of his ever more sober drawings, from *Vollard*, 1915, to *Stravinsky*, 1920, the elegant research of 1918: *Mrs. Rosenberg and Her Daughter, Olga Picasso, Pierrot Sitting* and then to the fullness of the *Four Bathing Girls* of 1921.

As if to relax in the middle of his efforts he periodically returns to this conception, improving every time, especially in his innumerable engravings, in smiling easiness, in prestigious know-how, in attractive freedom of line: from the portraits of *Paul*, 1923 and 1924, undoubtedly lovingly painted, the delicate *Harlequins* or *Woman in White* of 1924, the admirable engravings for Ovid's *Metamorphosis*, in 1930, for *Lysistrata* by Aristophanes in 1934, or the aquatints for *The Natural History* by D. Buffon, up to the bitter humor of the hundred-eighty drawings of *The Old Painter and His Model* (1953-54) and the portraits of *Jacqueline* in 1954 or *The Arlésienne*, 1958.

As soon as he was mature Picasso avoided figurative or descriptive painting to replace it by successive transpositions and thus entered a world of suggestion, an entirely recreated world ruled by the sole needs of plastic and expression. Arrived at the stage where elision, carried to its maximum, reaches the limit of pure abstraction but can also rejoin with a new materialisation independent of the initial theme, Picasso is master of his creation. In his effort to obtain the full participation of his being, he is obliged unceasingly to renew this universe which has been created by his hands and not through his imagination; and as we shall see, by leaning on a rigorous organization of a system of references and arbitrary equivalences with reality will bear the imprint of his prodigious personality.

III

UNITY UNDER APPEARANCE OF MULTIPLICITY

Everything depends on oneself...
The work one does is a way of keeping a diary.
PICASSO

Behind this prolix, multiform work of which the contours are so difficult to outline and the plastic intentions so hard to decipher, is profiled the silhouette of the creator who could stamp it with the indubitable mark of his powerful personality. Seldom has an artist been capable of expressing himself in such a direct an sincere manner. Trying to get closer to him in order to interpret his inner being, shall we eventually attain a better understanding of his efforts? But who, even among Picasso's closest friends and family can boast of a thorough knowledge of the artist?

The press and movies have so multiplied his portrait that here we only need to trace its essential characteristics. Anyhow, we still find him in the 1950s, hardly marked by time exactly as he depicted himself with such penetrating keenness in his *Self-Portrait* of 1906; the years have only thinned his hair and wrinkled his ample forehead. As in so many of the faces he painted, what first strikes one are those huge, deep-set eyes which dominate the whole face, illuminate and give it amazing animation. His gaze watches and flashes, leaps and seizes at a glance, bores for a moment the better to grasp and search fully, and then evades with a constant lively vivacity. The body and especially the hands participate in this extraordinary ballet, follow the same unceasing movements, quick, lithe and sure seeming to belong to a constantly alert feline or one about to spring.

Obviously the man who lives hidden behind these first impressions can only be approached with difficulty from outside. If he likes to be constantly surrounded by noise and the warmth of many living beings, human or animal, and though his friendship is effusive, nevertheless one feels him vigilant, almost jealous in guarding his solitude and his work, thus to avoid possible interference from those to whom

Antibes, 1946. Black lead

66

The Judgment of Paris, 1951.   Pen and ink.   Collection of the artist

he has given friendship and confidence.   This characteristic is due to a habit acquired when he was starting to work.

To his faithful friend Sabartès whom he sees daily he gives only a few glimpses of memories in the midst of conversation, and still less frequently some thoughts about his art.   To those who try and question him he answers by questions or frees himself from answering by a pirouette, or laughs them off with a joke.   Nevertheless when he wants to Picasso can disarm anyone by his instinctive authority, his quiet breeziness, and his welcoming kindness.   None of those who really have known him can resist the influence of his untiring curiosity, his knowledge, which seems inexhaustible in the most various fields, or his brilliant intelligence and scintillating memory.

I shared his friendship on the solitary beaches of Golfe Juan, as well as at the table (simple in these days) of the "Catalan," and more often in the garret of the Rue des Grands Augustins in the darkest

5 juillet 46

Young Girl, 1946.   Black-lead drawing.   Antibes

PORTRAIT OF MADAME Z, 1954. Oil, 39⅜″ × 31⅞″ (100 × 81 cm). Collection of the artist

PORTRAIT OF MAÏA (Daughter of the Artist), 1938.   Oil, 29″ × 24″ (73.7 × 61 cm).   Collection of the artist

PORTRAIT OF SYLVETTE, 1954. Oil, 50″ × 39″ (121 × 99 cm). Private collection

Portrait of Paloma, 1952. Pen and ink. Collection of the artist

◁

PORTAIT OF MADAME H. P., 1952
Oil, 64″ × 42″ (162.5 × 106.5 cm)
Private collection

7 juin 43

The Artist's Daughter, Wearing a Doll in Her Hair, 1943.   Black lead.   Paris

Head of a Woman, 1942.   India ink and gouache.   Paris

days of the German occupation of Paris, at the time of truth which had freed him from his traditional court of parasites and the curious, when our group, reduced in numbers day by day, would come to seek comfort from his lucid courage and incisive irony, and I can affirm that he never thought of playing a role but lived naturally, completely, with a spirit of total independence. As a matter of fact we can see him later posing for the cameras with the same humorous unaffectedness and proud assurance. To those who with an evident lack of good faith have never ceased to interpret his attitude as a desire on his part ot show off or mystify, it should be said that this mixture of extreme guardedness and pride is essentially a Spanish trait which is very strong in Picasso. After almost sixty years of Parisian life I hope no objective mind would deny him the right and merit owed him in the development of French contemporary painting, of which he has been since the beginning an integrating part and a major feature. He has known how to take the best out of this atmosphere and the pictorial inheritance which were offered to him in order to guide his research, logically organize his conquests, damp down and dominate his impulses and force himself, whenever necessary, to a certain degree of restraint. However, he remained essentially Spanish in his way of life as well as by temperament. From having lived during many years in close communion with the spirit of Spain, or more exactly with the inheritance Spain has left across the Atlantic, it is probably easier for me to understand the typical ways of this Hispanism, which, in my opinion, constitutes the basis of Picasso's art. If one takes this into consideration, his work is seen under a different light and can be explained even in its most peculiar aspects.

The Continuous Amorous Flamenco

Without entirely sharing the somewhat too dogmatic opinion of Kahnweiler who says, "his subjects are his loves," it must be admitted that the artist himself confirms that women occupy an exceptional place in his world for he says "At the end there is nothing but love." It would be scarcely an exaggeration, though not perhaps quite seemly, to try to divide and classify his production in relation to the main love affairs of his life. Without indulging in gossip, his most careful biographers have been unable to avoid noting and establishing a close parallel between his every new sentimental adventure and a fresh aesthetic outlook. Sabartès himself said quite rightly: "The shocks marking the amorous periods of his life can always be felt in his work, for Picasso, with his impulsive temperament, is incapable of keeping his secrets to himself." He does not hide any of his affairs and one could indeed trace the various moments of enthusiasm or of disillusion which have preceded or followed his successive meetings with Fernande Olivier in 1905, Marcelle Humbert, called Eva or My Pretty One, in 1912, Olga Moklova, whom he married in 1918 and who will bear him a son named Paul in 1921, Marie-Thérèse Walter in 1931 who will give birth to Maïa in 1935, Dora Maar in 1936, Françoise Gillot whose children, Claude and Paloma, will be born in 1947 and 1949, and Jacqueline Roquer in 1954.

But everything betrays a conception, a way of acting specifically Spanish. He scarcely thinks of painting a portrait of the object of his passionate attention; or else he presents her under unfavorable aspects, hides her under disguises, or evokes her in anonymous nudes in the same way that he hides his love, at its beginnings, far from any indiscreet eye.

As in the Flamenco figures — the traditional dance of his native Andalusia — during the period which Sabartès so justly called "the great parade to win her heart," Picasso is seen acting a true mimic of seduction, introducing in his painting a sweeping tenderness of line and gracious inflections; then soon he gives in to happy exaltation. Works then multiply with extraordinary ease as for instance in the

MEDITERRANEAN LANDSCAPE, 1952
Oil, 32″ × 49⅛″ (81.3 × 124.7 cm)
Private collection

CAFÉ IN ROYAN, 1940
Oil, 37¹³/₁₆″ × 51¼″ (96 × 130 cm)
Private collection

◁

THE TURKISH SHAWL
Oil, 51″ × 37½″ (129.5 × 95.3 cm)
Louise Leiris Gallery, Paris

WOMEN OF ALGIERS (After Delacroix), 1955
Oil, 45″ × 50″ (114.3 × 127 cm)
Collection of the artist

period the *Joie de Vivre*, 1946. At other times dance around the eternal feminine becomes a vibrating tension, an imposing haughtiness, or on the contrary takes on the form of a tormenting obsession reflecting savage sensuality and desire which comes out in the arabesques, the quality of the color or attributes of virility, such as in the series of *The Minotaur*, 1933 or *The Centaur*, 1946-47. When some painful separation occurs he is prostrated, sometimes incapable of painting for several months, seeking compensating liberation in poetry, drawing or engraving which are more rapid mediums and in which he can express his disappointment or misery whith bitter irony, as in the large series *The Old Painter and His Model*, 1953-1954. The superb violence of these emotional transports and their deep influence on the whole development of his artistic creation, have lead some people to call his work expressionist. But these frenzied outbursts have nothing in common with the impetuous transports of a Chaim Soutine or an Oskar Kokoschka letting themselves be carried away by their own lyricism. There is nothing unwarranted or arbitrary in this long monologue of the artist with himself, this confession in turn ardent or moving which reveals the whole power of his nature.

The Two Guiding Poles: Passion and Mortification

To find an analogy with such an exceptional and dominating temperament one should turn again to the Spanish school and especially to Goya. Unlike Goya, however, who had to abide by the constraints of his time, Picasso is entirely unconstrained, having at an early age rejected shackles or conventions in order to liberate this thirst for life which burns in him and overflows from his very being. He is only careful to harness it to the needs of art without thwarting its thrust and power of expression. He uses this magnificently and manages to give the impression of never having sacrificed any part of an all-powerful impulsiveness. He lives in close familiarity with the beings he brought to life and the objects he has animated, as in times past during the world's genesis, with the various fantasms which he exorcizes and even with the crowd of gods which he liberates from their eternal frozen Olympus. Like a true peasant who feels happy in appraising and weighing his riches, one senses he is obsessed with the insatiable desire of possession; he thoroughly enjoys feeling and caressing with his fingers or his eye the innumerable component parts of his creation. But he does not loiter overmuch for his overflowing vitality prevents him from attaching himself or settling down for long. Every moment his attention is occupied somewhere; he can choose among all the creatures, objects or techniques which his seeking curiosity makes him rediscover, always with the same amused bewilderment.

In this continuous treasure-hunt he is often happy with the smallest motive of interest which has caught his eye: unexpected still life, heteroclite material, old memories, precise suggestions or colored splashes, and gains from it a whole scale of possible variations, taking advantage of the temporary enthusiasm inspired by this encounter.

Everything is integrated and linked by an intimate feeling of human communion in a comprehensive universe, intermixed by the constant turmoil of fleeting or insistent passion in the midst of which he moves freely. There is, however, one constant — the Spanish civil war — the events of which will reveal the deep-rooted unconditional love he has for his country.

To stem such a flow and to avoid its degenerating into a superficial elation, being a true Mediterranean, Picasso has at his disposal another recourse which maintains his expression in the indispensable tone of sternness and dignity: the inherent feeling of fatality. Due to an old atavism which probably comes from an Islamic heritage, the presence of death always coincide with the taste for life which he has brought to its paroxysm. In his mind there is no escape. It is a tacit acceptance and, as in a bullfight,

Villa at Vallauris, 1952.   Pen and ink.   Louise Leiris Gallery, Paris

he will follow the risks right to the end.   His existence itself is narrowed to a closed field and we can note how landscapes as well as his interiors already evoke a strictly restricted space where the frequent adding of a mirror recalls the idea of a game without any possible illusion, of an impassable barrier. How often he represents this desperate fight for life — symbolized by a horse, a candle, a bull, a child — against the dark, beastlike forces of anihilation while a number of his paintings also evoke, through other means, this fundamental antagonism.   His whole work is interspersed, as in a daily ritual, with death-signs with which he juggles, one would almost say with pleasure: skulls, bucrania, death's-heads, triangular signs multiplied to excess and as sharp as many daggers, processions of lamenting women and constant parades of masked faces often resembling penitents.   To those who would like to pretend that this staging merely responds to some gruesome humor or to the desire to shock, let us remind them that very often, during the war periods, it has acquired its full significance and becomes a prophetic warning, a tragic accusation, an agonized protest in the face of the world.

Picasso likes to persevere in this attitude of mortification which Valdès Léal would not have disavowed. During certain periods he even goes so far as to give up the attraction of color, to sacrifice to the austerity of camaïeu or black and white.   Faithful servant of Hispanic tradition that he is, he professes a kind of sacred respect for anything distorted, monstrous, horrible or cruel and on occasion details it with relish, as for example in the repeated theme of a disemboweled horse.

Woman especially is frequently metamorphosed — except mother and child which rank as symbols of pity and redemption — into blasphemous figures which seem to resuscitate the most ancient images of menacing mother-goddesses or fierous Erinyes and become the absolute antithesis of so many attractive nymphs or naiads created by these same hands.

During his whole creative life Picasso has thus refused to choose, preferring to let himself respond to the pulse of his own life with its dark obsessions and its hopes, always swinging between the ebbing and flowing, torn between these two poles which consitute the axis of human condition.

Bull in Pasture, 1952.   Ink drawing.   Private collection, Lyons

Studio Scene, 1953.   Pen and ink

Woman and Monkey, 1954.   Pen and ink.   Galerie Louise Leiris, Paris

Bullfight, 1957.   Pen and ink.   Louise Leiris Gallery, Paris

THE MUDEJAR ENGRAVER

Among many other characteristic aspects of Picasso's art, the connection with his Iberian heritage should be underlined.   It is this extraordinary graphic virtuosity, which he says he could already boast of even as a child in front of his sisters, when on the sand beaches of Malaga.   Fifty years later, he can demonstrate the same extraordinary ability, this time before a photographer for "Life" who asked him to start at any place on a surface and finish a drawing, without even needing to look at it; in this particular performance his hand was only holding an electric torch.

His ability to make use so freely of various graphic techniques, the wealth of his production in all these fields: illustrations, engravings, lithographs, drawings, the sureness, the flexibility, the living aspect and the extreme agility of any of these are so obvious, that even his worst enemies could not help but grant him the title and rank — so well-deserved — of the greatest draftsman of the century. His best form of expression is in his line which answers exactly his need for spontaneity, even in his painting, where it almost always constitutes the main element.

But in our opinion, Picasso has another quality still more peculiar and interesting. Apollinaire was the first to detect this, followed by some of his best biographers such as Wilhelm Boeck. With his undeniable perspicacity he wrote: "By his mind he is more a Latin, by his rhythm more an Arab." His line is so personal, it gushes majestically, winds, undulates, retracts, or leaps forth as if self-intoxicated, sometimes ends in inextricable lace-work and indeed corresponds to artistic conceptions which are closer to Islam than to the West.

From his maternal ancestry, from the fire which is in him as well as from his physical appearance, Picasso could hardly deny his Andalusian origin. Why not, then, admit that he has received this special capacity

Bullfight, 1957. Ink and wash drawing

as a hereditary gift from Andalusian goldsmiths through some biological resurgence. His ability to let a line flow recalls the Mudejar style which has been perpetuated down to our times through the handicraft traditions of Spain. In several canvases of the Cubist period, even more in those painted from 1938 on which bring to mind certain fiber weavings: *Men or Women with Lollipop*, *Sitting Women* and in certain similar drawings, or in *The Demoiselles on the Banks of the Seine*, 1950, he seems to have undertaken real damask work.

One will especially note in all his work — and developing even more during the last fifteen years — a close parallel with the main convention of Moslem art: the same horror for emptiness; the same need to fill the whole surface of his canvases through means of multiple distortions of objects or beings and density of structures repeating up to infinity. There is also the frequent habit — which Sabartès noticed — of including inscriptions or writings — even when it is only his own signature — in his mural paintings, his canvases and his drawings, which has a curious analogy with the tradition of Andalusian cursive script.

Without wanting to involve a determinism which our times only accepts with difficulty, one can suppose, and not be far from wrong, that when the ten year old Pablo left Malaga with the same nostalgia that his father had (he will go back there from time to time) he took with him, and forever, the memories of the gardens and patios of Alcazaba and of so many other places. Later on he will often enjoy bringing back to life on his canvases the enchanting blue of the azueros or the mysterious blossoming of geometrical crisscrosses which had illuminated his early childhood and which will always feed his work.

IV

IN THE STEPS OF THE CENTURY

I always have painted for my time...
Painting no longer is a manufacture, it
has become a creation and thus has
forever ceased to be comfortable.

PICASSO

As time has gone by, Picasso's work has increasingly taken on its authentic greatness, its significance full of painful worries, its true human tune. Just as had happened for the Impressionists, Picasso's work seemed for a long time purposeless to his immediate contemporaries, without any bearing on current events, showing no internal logic and born from whim and extravagance; it was also accused of solely mocking and mystifying the public, of being "a pure invention of speculation."

But it took root in its time with such convincing authority that even now it is unanimously considered as one of its most faithful emanations. It even managed to mold the epoch entirely to its own image. Not without irony, its author could already claim during the first world war that the army in starting camouflage had acknowledged Cubism's reasoning. Today this form of art has triumphantly penetrated everywhere. Its imprint has marked the whole interior and out-of-doors decorations of our lives and there is hardly a field which has not borrowed at least a part of its aesthetic principles. Its influence has even expanded to the whole world. Seldom has an artist had such a wide audience.

It would, however, be unfair not to include all those who took part, at Picasso's side, in this glorious march of modern art. Georges Braque, Henri Laurens, Juan Gris and so many others which sometimes have been more directly involved such as Fernand Léger, or have widened some of the problems he had set down: Robert Delaunay, Robert Mondrian, Vassily Kandinsky, the Futurists, Jacques Villon, etc... not forgetting the artists of the new generation who, from Francisco Borès to Edward Pignon, from Hans Hartung to Alfred Manessier, have known how to reap — each in his own way — the best of his heritage.

How come, then that Picasso continues, after so many years, to still be on the front of the artistic stage and to have such a strong influence? It is because he obviously is the only one among his companions to have unceasingly walked in the steps of the century and even often to have gone ahead of them. We can find the equivalent of every stage he went through, of each one of his new styles in the general evolution of the epoch. One could draw a close parallel between the various periods of his research and the great contemporary currents which awake so many echoes in his productions. There is hardly a label that would not fit him for he explored every possibility: Nabi, Fauve, primitive, Cubist, Constructivist; abstract, naive, Surrealist, Expressionist, and was in turn the rival of Braque, Matisse and so many others. It matters little whether he has or not initiated several aesthetic movements,

PAINTED POTTERY PLATE, 1948

whether he preceded or followed them for, with an amazing faculty for assimilation, he has managed to melt every form of expression into his strong personality and to give each a decisive turn. His work has always been in the center of the epoch's worries and has managed to represent them with an admirable foreknowledge.

Surely his violence and exaggeration evoke in a suggestive way this exasparated individualism — of which Picasso is the most faithful interpreter — forcefully rebelling against the ever-growing powers of coercion and uniformization. In the same way the constant unsatisfaction ruling all his life translates the permanent revolt of individualism faced with an aggressive materialsm, the need to seek refuge in his own creation and to save a certain spiritual enjoyment.

Closely mingling the concrete and the imaginary, going alternatively from one to the other without any difficulty, expanding an object's existence far off into dream and thus associating microcosm and macrocosm, Picasso resets man into this new universe which from day to day seems limitless both in its smallest and largest dimension. The diversity of the spaces which he recreated by inventing them for almost every one of his painted, carved or engraved work is the true image of these horizons which every discovery enlarges up to the immeasurable.

The evidence of all the phenomena of simultaneous vision which he has registered and the transformations he brought into the relationship space-time is an exact prefiguration of a near future already used in television. Can this mechanized-looking world submitted to a rough rhythm which he made his for so long be considered today as a daring anticipation in an era where mechanism and speed prevail? And finally by emphasizing again with such mastery the wealth of instinctive forces did he not open to artistic expression every door of the future and allowed it to immerse again in the human heart on the level of a real universalism?

His art may appear inhuman to those who have not yet understood that we live at an inhuman period; we should remind them that we have, alas, been witness to visions from the Apocalypse being converted into every day's reality.

Where others only take care of not getting involved Picasso, who has always suffered all the miseries engendered by wars, never hesitated to express his pitiful premonitions in his art. Because of this passionate and tragic feeling for life which he carries in him he was able, far before Existentialism, before the plays of Beckett or Ionesco, to interpret the anguish of man before his destiny which has dominated our contemporary world, with all its immensity and dignity.

Young people have never been mistaken about his attitude and have felt a communion of thought with Picasso; for his part he has tried to maintain a contact with them. When during the darkest hours of German occupation I summoned them they all had the courage to come forward and acknowledge their debt and gratitude to him, facing the curses and threats of the Nazis and their knaves. And since the foundation of the Salon de Mai we can see every year a work of Picasso hanging among the new generation's paintings. This is the symbol of the spirit of renewal which always animated him and thanks to which he has been able, at every moment, to grasp the pathetic and secret face of our time and to force it into the conscience of all.

BIBLIOGRAPHY

GENERAL WORKS

CHRISTIAN ZERVOS, *Pablo Picasso*, Catalogue T. I à X (oeuvres de 1895 à 1940), Paris, Cahiers d'Art 1932 à 1959.

ALFRED H. BARR, Picasso, *Fifty years of his Art*, New-York, Museum of Modern Art, 1946.

FRANK ELGAR et ROBERT MAILLARD, *Picasso*, Paris, Fernand Hazan, 1955.

JAIME SABARTES et WILHELM BOECK, *Picasso*, Paris, Flammarion, 1955.

ANTONINA VALLENTIN, *Pablo Picasso*, Paris, Albin Michel, 1957.

BERNARD GEISER, *Picasso, peintre-graveur*, Berne 1933. Lausanne, Clairefontaine 1955.

FERNAND MOURLOT, *Picasso lithographe* (2 vol.), Monte-Carlo, Edit. du Livre, 1949-1950.

DANIEL-HENRY KAHNWEILER, *Les sculptures de Picasso*, Paris, Edit. du Chêne, 1949.

C. ZERVOS, J. SABARTES, MADOURA, *Les céramiques de Picasso*, Paris, Cahiers d'Art, 23e année no 1, 1948.

SELECTED WORKS

M. RAYNAL, *Picasso*, Paris, L'effort moderne, 1922.

J. COCTEAU, *Picasso*, Paris, Stock, 1923.

P. REVERDY, *Picasso*, Paris 1924.

W. GEORGE, *Picasso: Dessins*, Paris, Edit. des quatre Chemins, 1926.

C. ZERVOS, *Picasso, oeuvres 1920-26*, Paris, Cahiers d'Art 1927.

A. LEVEL, *Picasso*, Paris, Crès 1928.

W. UHDE, *Picasso et la tradition française*, Paris 1928.

H. MAHAUT, *Picasso*, Paris, Crès 1930.

E. D'ORS, *Picasso*, Paris, Edit. des Chroniques du Jour, 1930.

Hommage à Picasso, Paris, Revue "Documents", 2e Année no 3, 1930.

C. ZERVOS, *Picasso*, Paris, Cahiers d'Art 1932.

F. OLIVIER, *Picasso et ses amis*, Paris 1933.

C. ZERVOS, *Picasso*, Paris, Cahiers d'Art 1935.

G. DE TORRE, *Picasso*, Madrid 1936.

Picasso, Ténerife, "Gaceta de Arte", no 37, 1936.

J. SABARTES, *Picasso*, Milan 1937.

J. CASSOU, *Picasso*, Paris 1937.

Guernica, Paris, Cahiers d'Art no 4-5, 1937.

YOSHIO KITAHARA, *Picasso*, 54 Zeichnungen, Tokio 1937.

P. HAESAERTS, *Picasso et le goût du paroxysme*, Anvers-Amsterdam 1938.

GERTRUDE STEIN, *Picasso*, Paris, Floury 1938.

C. ZERVOS, *Picasso*, Paris, Cahiers d'Art no 3-10, 1938.

JEAN CASSOU, *Picasso*, Paris, Hypérion 1940 et 1946.

J. MERLI, *Picasso, el artista y la obra*, Buenos Aires 1942 et 1948.

ROBERT DESNOS, *Picasso, 16 peintures 1939-43*, Paris, Edit. du Chêne 1943.

E. PRAMPOLINI, *Picasso scultore*, Rome 1943.

R. GOMEZ DE LA SERNA, *Completa y veridica historia de Picasso y el cubismo*, Turin 1945.

JAIME SABARTES, *Picasso, portraits et souvenirs*, Paris, L. Carré et M. Vox 1946.

JAIME SABARTES, *Picasso*, Paris, Couleur des Maîtres, Braun 1946.

WILLIAM S. LIEBERMAN, *Picasso and the Ballet*, New York 1946.

D. SUTTON, *Picasso, époques bleue et rose*, Paris, Edit. du Chêne 1948.

J. SABARTES et P. ELUARD, *Picasso à Antibes*, Paris 1948.

S. et G. RAMIE, *Céramiques de Picasso*, Genève 1948.

T. TZARA, *Pablo Picasso*, Genève, Skira 1948.

C. ZERVOS, *Picasso à Antibes*, Paris, Cahiers d'Art no 19-20, 1948.

J. LASSAIGNE, *Picasso*, Paris 1949.

C. ZERVOS, *Dessins de Picasso*, 1892-1948, Paris, Cahiers d'Art 1949.

J. BOURET, *Picasso, dessins*, Paris, Edit. des Deux Mondes 1950.

ALEXANDRE CIRICI PELLICER, *Picasso avant Picasso*, Genève, Edit. P. Cailler 1950.

A. VERDET, *L'homme au mouton*, Paris 1950.

Picasso, oeuvres de 1937 à 1950, Tokio, Journal Yomiuri 1951.

MAURICE GIEURE, *Initiation à l'oeuvre de Picasso*, Paris, Edit. des Deux Mondes 1951.

ANDRE VERDET, *Pablo Picasso au Musée d'Antibes*, Paris, Edit. Falaize 1951.

P. ELUARD, *Picasso, dessins*, Paris 1952.

Picasso, Mulhouse, no XLII du Point, oct. 1952.

W. S. Lieberman, *Picasso: Blue and Rose Periods* New York 1952.

A. Verdet, *La chèvre de Picasso*, Paris, Edit. de Beaune 1952.

Maurice Raynal, *Picasso*, Lausanne, Skira 1953.

J. Sabartes, *Picasso ceramista*, Milan 1953.

Claude Roy, *Guerre et Paix*, Cercle d'Art 1953.

T. Tzara, *Picasso et la poésie*, Rome 1953.

Jaime Sabartes, *Picasso, documents iconographiques*, Genève, P. Cailler 1954.

Fernanda Wittgens, *Picasso*, Milan 1954.

Suite de 180 dessins de Picasso, 1953-54, Paris, Verve no 29-30, 1954.

Vercors, *Picasso, oeuvres des Musées de Léningrad et de Moscou*, Paris, Cercle d'Art 1955.

Roland Penrose, *Picasso*, Londres, Gollancz 1958.

J. Sabartes, *Les Ménines*, Paris, Cercle d'Art 1958.

Douglas Cooper, *Carnet Catalan*, Paris, Berggruen 1958. .

G. Boudaille, *Picasso, Carnet de Californie*, Paris, Cercle d'Art 1959.

Helene Parmelin, *Picasso sur la place*, Paris, Julliard 1959.

M. Jardot, *Picasso, dessins*, Paris, Calman Lévy 1959.

J. Cassou, *Picasso*, Paris, Somogy 1960.

J. Prevert, *Portraits de Picasso*, Milan, Muggiani 1960.

R. Cogniat, *Picasso, figures*, Paris, Bibliothèque des Arts 1960.

J. Sabartes, *Picasso, Faunes et flores d'Antibes*, Paris, Pont des Arts 1960.

ILLUSTRATIONS

Acrobat on a Ball 11
Antibes 66
Artist's Daughter, Wearing a Doll in Her Hair
(The) 74

Balcony (The) 33
Blind Man (The) 19
Boisgeloup 46, 47
Bullfight 10, 86, 87
Bull in Pasture 83

Café in Royan 79
Conversation (The) 56
Coq (Le) 49

Dove 64

Embrace (The) 14

Flower Seller (The) 5
Fruit Dish and Pitcher by the Window 59

Guernica 62-63

Harlequin and His Companion 12
Head of a Woman 17, 21, 39, 75
Head of a Young Man 38

Italian Girl 35

Journal. Collage (The) 32
Judgment of Pâris (The) 67

Landscape 51
Little Girl with a Basket of Flowers 15

Man with a Mandolin 30
Maternity 13
Mediterranean Landscape 77
Minotaur and His Prey 55

Painted Pottery Plate 90
Pierrot Sitting 34
Portrait of "Bibi la Purée" 24
Portrait of Madame H. P. 72
Portrait of Madame Z. 69
Portrait of Maïa (Daughter of the Artist) 70
Portrait of Paloma 73
Portrait of Sylvette 71
Portrait of the Son of the Artist as Pierrot .. 41

Reclining Nude 27, 45

Seated Nude 9, 16
Seated Woman 8, 29
Self-Portrait 3
Skull of a Bull 60
Skull of a Sheep 61
Still Life 36, 50, 58
Still Life with Bust and Palette 52
Still Life with Head of a Black Bull 57
Studio Scene 84
Study for the Demoiselles d'Avignon 22, 23

Three Acrobats (The) 37
Three Musicians (The) 43
Three-quarter Head 25
Turkisk Shawl 78
Two Harlequins 42

Villa at Vallauris 82
Violin and Flute 20

Waiting 6
Woman and Monkey 85
Woman Asleep: The Dream 44
Women of Algiers (After Delacroix) 80
Wounded Bird 31

Young Girl 53, 68

759.4
PICASSO